"From Novices to Pros: Pucking Around for All Skill Levels"

Rachel Lia

:Table of Contents.

Chapter 1: The Beginner's Puck Journey

Introduction:

Starting a trip in any sport can be both instigative and intimidating. The same holds true for those venturing into the world of ice hockey. The Beginner's Puck Journey is an disquisition into the fundamentals, challenges, and triumphs that await beginners to the sport. This comprehensive companion aims to give precious perceptivity and guidance for those taking their first way on the ice. From understanding the outfit to learning introductory chops, this trip will empower newcomers to make a solid foundation and set them on a path to getting complete hockey players.

The Call of the Ice
The first chapter of the Beginner's Puck Journey delves into the appeal of ice hockey. It explores the history and artistic

significance of the sport, pressing the passion and fellowship that compass it. Understanding the roots of the game can help newcomers develop a deeper appreciation and provocation for their own trip.

Essential outfit
Before stepping onto the ice, newcomers must familiarize themselves with the necessary outfit. This chapter provides an in- depth overview of each piece, including skates, helmet, pads, and sticks. It emphasizes the significance of proper fit, safety considerations, and recommended brands for newcomers.

Getting to Know the Rink
The ice rink can feel like a foreign home to newcomers, but this chapter demystifies its layout and language. Exploring the colorful zones, lines, and markings, newcomers will gain a clear understanding of the playing face and its significance during the game.

learning the Basics
structure a strong foundation is pivotal for any freshman, and this chapter focuses on the abecedarian chops of ice

hockey. From literacy to grind and maintain balance to handling the stick and firing, newcomers will be guided step- by- step through each skill. Exercise drills and exercises are handed to help beginners develop proficiency.

cooperation and Communication
Ice hockey is a platoon sport that relies heavily on effective communication and cooperation. This chapter explores the significance of communication on the ice, from calling for passes to signaling plays. It also emphasizes the significance of trust, cooperation, and supporting teammates both on and off the ice.

Rules of the Game
Understanding the rules of ice hockey is essential for newcomers to share safely and effectively. This chapter covers the introductory rules and penalties, including offside, icing, and colorful contraventions. By grasping the rules, newcomers can navigate the game with confidence and avoid gratuitous penalties.

Strategies and Positioning
As newcomers gain a grasp of the game's fundamentals, this chapter introduces

strategies and positioning. Exploring descent and protective strategies, beginners will learn about forechecking, backchecking, and other tactics to gain an advantage on the ice. It also delves into the different positions and their places within a platoon.

structure Physical Fitness
Ice hockey demands physical fitness and exertion. This chapter provides guidance on developing strength, abidance, and dexterity through off- ice exercises and training routines. It also emphasizes the significance of nutrition and injury forestallment, helping newcomers maintain optimal performance.

Chancing a Community
Engaging with a community of fellow players and suckers is a pivotal aspect of the Beginner's Puck Journey. This chapter explores ways to connect with original leagues, brigades, and training programs. It also discusses the benefits of joining hockey communities, including mentorship, support, and participated gests .

Overcoming Challenges

The Beginner's Puck Journey isn't without its obstacles. This chapter addresses common challenges faced by newcomers, similar as fear of falling, lack of confidence, and frustration. Practical tips and strategies are handed to help beginners overcome these hurdles and stay motivated on their path to enhancement.

Chapter 2: Skating Towards Skill Acquisition

Introduction:

Skating is the foundation of ice hockey, and learning this abecedarian skill is essential for players of all positions and skill situations. Skating Towards Skill Acquisition explores the art and fashion of groaning in ice hockey, furnishing comprehensive perceptivity, tips, and exercises to help players ameliorate their skating capacities. From proper station and balance to speed and dexterity, this companion will claw into the crucial rudiments of skating and give guidance on how to acquire and upgrade these chops.

The significance of Skating in Ice Hockey

Skating isn't only a means of transportation on the ice; it's the backbone of the sport. This section emphasizes the significance of strong skating chops in ice hockey, pressing the impact on speed, project, and overall performance. It also discusses how proper skating fashion enables players to execute other chops effectively.

Understanding the Mechanics of Skating
Before diving into specific skating ways, it's pivotal to understand the mechanics behind effective and important strides. This section breaks down the different factors of skating, including weight distribution, push- offs, glide phases, and recovery movements. By comprehending the mechanics, players can develop a further conscious and purposeful approach to their skating fashion.

Achieving Proper station and Balance
A strong foundation begins with a proper station and balance. This section focuses on the body position, knee bend, and center of graveness necessary for optimal balance and stability. It provides drills and exercises to help players develop a solid base, which in turn

enhances their capability to induce power and initiative effectively on the ice.

Generating Power and Speed
Speed is a pivotal asset in ice hockey, and this section explores ways for generating power and adding skating speed. motifs covered include stride length, quick thresholds, explosive acceleration, and effective weight transfer. colorful drills and exercises are handed to help players enhance their power and speed on the ice.

Enhancing dexterity and swiftness
dexterity and swiftness are essential for maneuvering through tight spaces, escaping opponents, and executing quick changes in direction. This section focuses on ways similar as crossovers, pivots, side movements, and edge control. Players will learn how to ameliorate their dexterity and swiftness through specific drills and exercises that target these chops.

learning Transitions and Turns
Smooth and effective transitions and turns are crucial rudiments of effective skating in ice hockey. This section covers ways for executing flawless transitions

between forward and backward skating, as well as tight turns and pivots. Players will learn to develop better body control, weight stirring, and edge application to execute these movements effectively.

Skating with Puck Control
Skating while maintaining control of the elf adds an fresh subcaste of complexity to the game. This section provides perceptivity on maintaining proper body position, balance, and collaboration while handling the elf. It also offers drills and exercises that combine skating and elf control to help players ameliorate their capability to grind confidently with the elf.

Expanding Skating Chops Advanced ways
Once players have developed a solid foundation in skating, they can begin to explore more advanced ways. This section introduces chops similar as backwards groaning, backward crossovers, mohawks, and other advanced pushes. It provides step- by- step instructions and practice drills to help players gradationally acquire and upgrade these chops.

Mental Aspects of Skating

Skating proficiency isn't solely dependent on physical capacities; internal aspects also play a pivotal part. This section explores the internal factors that impact skating, including focus, expectation, and confidence. It offers strategies for maintaining internal countenance and developing a strong mindset to enhance skating performance.

Training and Practice Routines

To truly exceed in skating, players must devote regular time to training and practice. This section provides guidance on structuring training sessions and practice routines specifically acclimatized to perfecting skating chops. It emphasizes the significance of thickness, reiteration, and incorporating skating drills into overall training plans.

Chapter 3: Stick Handling 101: Basics and Beyond

Introduction:

Stick running is an essential skill in ice hockey, allowing players to control the elf, initiative through opponents, and produce scoring openings. Stick Handling 101 Basics and Beyond is a comprehensive companion that explores the fundamentals of stick running and provides in- depth perceptivity and ways to help players ameliorate their elf control capacities. From proper hand positioning and stick grip to advanced dekes and fakes, this companion will take players on a trip from the basics to more advanced stick running chops.

The significance of Stick Handling in Ice Hockey

Stick running is a abecedarian skill that directly impacts a player's capability to maintain possession, make accurate passes, and execute scoring plays. This section emphasizes the significance of stick running in ice hockey and highlights how learning this skill can elevate a player's overall performance on the ice.

Understanding Stick and Hand Positioning
Proper stick and hand positioning form the foundation of effective stick running. This section explores the optimal grip on the stick, hand placement, and the significance of inflexibility and dexterity. Players will learn how to achieve a balanced and controlled station that allows for maximum control and project.

Controlling the Puck Basic ways
This section focuses on the introductory ways used to control the elf while stick running. It covers essential chops similar as the forehand and cacography tittle, elf gates, and simple pushes to cover the elf from opponents. Players will learn how to maintain a soft touch on the stick, allowing for precise elf control and quick response times.

Developing elf mindfulness
elf mindfulness is pivotal for successful stick running. This section delves into ways and drills that help players develop a jacked sense of the elf's position and movement. It explores the significance of supplemental vision, head positioning, and expectation, allowing players to make quick opinions and reply effectively in different game situations.

Advanced Stick Handling ways
Once players have learned the basics, they can expand their stick handling force with further advanced ways. This section introduces chops similar as the toe drag, between- the- legs moves, and one- handed stick running. It provides step- by- step instructions, practice drills, and vidcotape demonstrations to help players precipitously develop their proficiency in executing these advanced pushes.

Deception and Fakes
The capability to deceive opponents through fakes and dekes is a precious skill in stick running. This section explores colorful deking ways, including the shoulder fake, toe drag deke, and the

notorious" Forsberg move." Players will learn how to read opponents, produce space, and subsidize on scoring openings by effectively using deception in stick running.

Stick Handling in Game Situations
Effective stick handling in game situations requires rigidity and quick decision- timber. This section focuses on scripts similar as one- on- one battles, obnoxious rushes, and cycling the elf in the obnoxious zone. It provides strategies, tips, and practice drills to help players ameliorate their stick running chops in high- pressure game scripts.

perfecting Hand- Eye Coordination
Hand- eye collaboration is a pivotal aspect of stick running. This section explores exercises and drills that enhance hand- eye collaboration, including response drills, juggling exercises, and target- grounded training. By perfecting hand- eye collaboration, players can elevate their capability to track the elf, make accurate passes, and execute precise stick handling moves.

Stick Handling Off the Ice

To maximize stick running chops, players can condense their on- ice training with out- ice practice. This section provides suggestions for out- ice stick handling drills, including ball or elf handling with a stickhandling ball or golf ball. It also discusses the benefits of incorporating out- ice stick handling training into a comprehensive training routine.

Developing Stick Handling Creativity
Stick running isn't only about executing specific ways; it also involves developing creativity and extemporization. This section encourages players to experiment with their stick running, try new moves, and develop their own unique style. It emphasizes the significance of creativity in creating scoring openings and surprising opponents.

Chapter 4: Mastering the Art of Passing

Introduction:

Passing is a abecedarian skill in ice hockey that plays a pivotal part in platoon play, elf possession, and creating scoring openings. learning the Art of Passing is a comprehensive companion that explores the complications of passing in ice hockey, furnishing detailed perceptivity, ways, and strategies to help players ameliorate their passing capacities. From the basics of proper grip and hand positioning to advanced ways like goblet passes and tape recording- to- tape recording perfection, this companion will claw into the crucial rudiments of passing and empower players to come complete passers on the ice.

The significance of Passing in Ice Hockey

Passing is the backbone of effective cooperation and plays a vital part in the inflow and success of the game. This section emphasizes the significance of passing in ice hockey, pressing how accurate and well- timed passes can open up scoring openings, maintain possession, and keep opponents off balance.

Understanding the Basics Grip and Hand Positioning
A solid foundation in passing begins with proper grip and hand positioning on the stick. This section explores the optimal grip, hand placement, and body positioning necessary for accurate and controlled passes. Players will learn how to induce power and control by exercising the correct grip and hand positioning ways.

Developing Vision and Awareness
Passing requires excellent vision and mindfulness of teammates' positions on the ice. This section focuses on perfecting supplemental vision, surveying the ice, and anticipating teammates' movements. Players will learn how to read the play and make smart opinions to execute precise passes to their intended targets.

learning the Forehand Pass

The forehand pass is the most generally used pass in ice hockey. This section covers the ways and mechanics of the forehand pass, including weight transfer, follow- through, and proper release points. Players will learn how to induce accurate and crisp forehand passes across colorful distances and game situations.

unleashing the Backhand Pass

The cacography pass is a precious tool in a player's passing magazine, furnishing versatility and the capability to make passes in tight spaces. This section explores the mechanics and ways of the cacography pass, including body positioning, blade control, and wrist snap. Players will learn how to execute effective and accurate cacography passes to surprise opponents and maintain elf possession.

Advanced Passing ways Saucer Pass and Beyond

This section introduces advanced fleeting ways, starting with the goblet pass. Players will learn the mechanics of the goblet pass, which involves heaving the elf in a controlled manner over obstacles. also, this section covers other advanced end ways similar as bank passes, drop passes, and touch passes. It provides step- by- step instructions and practice drills to help players develop proficiency in these advanced end chops.

Timing and delicacy
Timing and delicacy are essential aspects of successful end. This section focuses on developing the capability to lead teammates with passes, delivering the elf to their intended destination with perfection. It explores ways similar as leading passes, goblet passes for upstanding event, and timing passes to exploit opponents' protective positioning. Players will learn how to enhance their passing delicacy through practice drills and game situations.

Passing in Different Game Situations
Passing isn't a one- size- fits- all skill; it must be acclimated to colorful game situations. This section covers end strategies in different game scripts, including rout passes, odd- man rushes, power plays, and cycling in the obnoxious zone. Players will learn how to make

effective opinions and execute well- timed passes to exploit protective gaps and produce scoring openings.

Communication andNon-Verbal Cues
Effective communication is vital in successful end. This section explores the significance ofnon-verbal cues, similar as eye contact, body language, and stick positioning, to establish effective end connections with teammates. It emphasizes the value of clear communication to enhance cooperation and insure accurate passes in high-pressure game situations.

Improving Passing Creativity
Passing isn't just about executing routine passes; it also involves creativity and extemporization. This section encourages players to experiment with different fleeting ways, try unanticipated passes, and develop their own unique end styles. It emphasizes the significance of creativity in surprising opponents and creating scoring openings.

Chapter 5: Shooting for Success: Aiming and Accuracy

Introduction:

Firing is a skill that requires perfection, focus, and thickness. Whether it's archery, target firing, or any other form of firing, aiming and delicacy are essential rudiments for achieving success. In this comprehensive companion, we will claw into the complications of aiming and delicacy, exploring the colorful factors that contribute to these chops and furnishing practical tips to help you ameliorate your firing proficiency. So, let's embark on a trip to discover the secrets behind shooting for success!

Understanding Aiming

Aiming is the process of aligning the armament or gunshot with the intended target. It involves a combination of visual perception, hand- eye collaboration, and internal focus. Then are some crucial factors to consider when it comes to aiming

Sight Alignment Proper sight alignment is pivotal for accurate firing. This refers to the alignment of the front and hinder sights of a arm or the aiming device in archery. The frontal sight should be centered and position with the hinder sight, allowing for a clear sight picture.

Eye Dominance Understanding your dominant eye is vital for shooting delicacy. utmost people have one eye that naturally takes priority over the other when it comes to visual input. Determining your dominant eye ensures that you align your sights rightly and concentrate on the target with lesser clarity.

Breath Control Maintaining control over your breath is essential for aiming stability. Firing during the natural respiratory pause, when your lungs are shortly empty, reduces body movement and increases perfection. Exercise breathing ways to enhance your firing thickness.

Enhancing delicacy
delicacy is the capability to constantly hit the intended target. While aiming sets the foundation, there are colorful other factors that impact delicacy. Let's explore some crucial aspects to concentrate on for perfecting delicacy

station and Body Position A stable and balanced firing station is pivotal for delicacy. Whether you are standing, kneeling, or prone, insure your body is aligned with the target, distributing your weight unevenly. This provides a solid foundation, minimizing unwanted movement during the shot.

Grip and Control Maintaining a establishment and harmonious grip on the armament or arc is essential for delicacy. insure that your grip is neither too tight nor too loose, allowing for proper control and flinch operation. Exercise dry blasting to upgrade your grip and detector control without live security.

Detector Control The moment of blasting is critical for delicacy. learning detector control involves applying steady, indeed pressure to the detector without disturbing the sight alignment. Avoid jerking or recoiling, as these can significantly affect delicacy. Regular dry blasting exercises can help upgrade this skill.

Follow- through Follow- through refers to maintaining the correct firing position after the shot is fired. This is frequently overlooked but plays a pivotal part in delicacy. Avoid anticipating the flinch or incontinently shifting your focus to the target. rather, maintain your position and concentrate until the shot sequence is complete.

Factors Affecting Aiming and Accuracy Several external factors can impact aiming and delicacy. Being apprehensive of these factors allows you to acclimatize and make necessary adaptations. Some significant factors to consider are

Environmental Conditions Weather conditions, similar as wind, rain, or extreme temperatures, can significantly affect shooting delicacy. Learn to compensate for windage and elevation adaptations, use wind flags or pointers, and practice firing under colorful rainfall conditions to ameliorate rigidity.

Equipment Quality The quality and condition of your firing outfit can impact delicacy. insure that your arm, bow, or other firing tools are well- maintained and duly calibrated. Regularly check for any wear and tear and gash or blights that may hamper your firing performance.

Distance and Target Size The distance between you and the target, as well as the target's size, affects the position of difficulty in aiming and delicacy. Firing at longer distances requires more precise aiming adaptations, while lower targets demand enhanced focus and perfection.

Mental Preparedness Firing isn't only a physical skill but also a internal bone . Developing a focused and disciplined mindset is pivotal for harmonious delicacy. Learn to manage stress, maintain attention, and fantasize successful shots. Mental exercises, similar as contemplation and visualization, can enhance your firing performance.

Practice and Training
Improving aiming and delicacy requires devoted practice and training. Then are some tips to help you enhance your firing chops

Regular Practice thickness is crucial. Set away devoted time for regular firing practice. Work on different aspects, similar as aiming, grip, detector control, and follow- through. Gradationally increase the difficulty position by challenging yourself with varying distances, targets, and shooting positions.

Seek Professional Guidance Matriculate the help of professional coaches or educated shooters who can give guidance, correct your fashion, and offer substantiated tips for enhancement. Their moxie can significantly accelerate your progress and help you overcome any firing challenges.

dissect and Reflect After each firing session, take time to dissect your performance. Identify areas where you bettered and areas that need enhancement. Keep a firing journal to track your progress, record compliances, and set specific pretensions for unborn training sessions.

Mental Conditioning Incorporate internal exertion ways into your training routine. Exercise internal exercises, fantasize successful shots, and develop a positive mindset. Mental adaptability and focus can greatly enhance your firing performance.

Chapter 6: Defensive Strategies for Novices

Introduction:

For neophyte individualities, learning and enforcing effective protective strategies is pivotal for particular safety and security. Whether you're concerned about your particular well- being or seeking to cover your loved bones
, understanding the basics of protective strategies can significantly enhance your capability to handle potentially dangerous situations. In this comprehensive companion, we will claw into the details of protective strategies for beginners, covering essential generalities, practical tips, and mindset medication to help you develop a solid foundation in particular defense.

Situational mindfulness

Situational mindfulness is the foundation of any effective protective strategy. It involves being alert and conscious of your surroundings, relating implicit pitfalls, and making informed opinions grounded on the situation. Then are crucial aspects of situational mindfulness

awareness Stay present and attentive to your terrain, avoiding distractions similar as mobile bias. Develop the habit of surveying your surroundings, assessing people's geste
, and relating implicit peril signs.

Environmental Factors Take note of factors similar as lighting, visibility, and the presence of security measures. Be apprehensive of the layout of the area, including possible exit routes and places of cover or concealment.

Gut Feeling Trust yourinstincts.However, it's essential to admit and respond to those passions, If commodity feels off or gives you a sense of apprehension. Suspicion can play a vital part in feting implicit pitfalls before they escalate.

Pre-Planning When visiting strange places, probe the position beforehand. Familiarize yourself with original crime rates, high- threat areas, and exigency services. This knowledge empowers you to make informed opinions and reduces the liability of chancing yourself in a dangerous situation.

Personal Security Measures
Incorporating particular security measures into your diurnal routine can greatly enhance your protective capabilities. Then are some abecedarian strategies to consider

Home Security insure your home is adequately secured. Install sturdy cinches on doors and windows, use a peephole or security camera to identify callers before opening the door, and consider using a home security system for added protection.

particular admonitions Carry a particular alarm that emits a loud noise when actuated. These small bias can attract attention and discourage implicit bushwhackers.

Lighting Maintain good lighting around your home, especially entrances and pathways. Acceptable lighting deters culprits and improves visibility, reducing the chances of getting a target.

tone- Defense Tools Familiarize yourself with legal tone- defense tools, similar as pepper spray, particular tasers, or particular admonitions. Learn how to use these tools effectively and exercise their deployment.

Verbal andNon-Physical Defense
Verbal andnon-physical defense ways are essential for diffusing potentially combative situations. Then are some strategies to consider

Verbal fierceness Develop strong verbal communication chops to assert yourself and establish boundaries. Use a confident and assertive tone while maintaining a regardful address. easily communicate your intentions and boundaries, expressing your reluctance to be a victim.

De-escalation In potentially unpredictable situations, concentrate onde-escalation rather than battle. Speak calmly, avoid aggression, and laboriously hear to the other person's enterprises. Find common ground and seek resolution without resorting to physical conflict.

Boundaries Understand and communicate particular boundaries effectively. Assertively and hypercritically state your limits and make it clear when someone has crossed them. By doing so, you establish prospects and discourage implicit raiders.

Avoidance and Escape Whenever possible, avoid potentially dangerous situationsaltogether.However, trust your instincts and remove yourself from the terrain, If you smell a trouble or suspect trouble. produce distance, seek backing, and prioritize your safety.

Physical tone- Defense ways
While physical tone- defense ways should be approached with caution, learning the basics can give an added subcaste of protection. Then are a many considerations

Basic Strikes and Techniques Enroll in a tone- defense course or martial trades class to learn abecedarian strikes, similar as punches, kicks, and knee strikes. also, concentrate on ways like blocking, escaping, and fighting attacks.

Target Areas Understanding the vulnerable areas of the mortal body can increase the effectiveness of your protective strikes. Aim for areas like the eyes, nose, throat, groin, and knees, as these are sensitive and can incapacitate an bushwhacker.

Exercise and Conditioning Regularly exercise your physical tone- defense ways to make muscle memory and increase confidence. Conditioning exercises, similar as strength training and cardiovascular exercises, ameliorate your overall fitness and stamina, enhancing your capability to defend yourself.

common Manipulation and Escapes Learn ways for common manipulation and escapes to free yourself from heists or holds. These ways can be effective in prostrating or disorienting an bushwhacker, furnishing you with an occasion to escape.

Mental and Emotional Preparedness
Preparing yourself mentally and emotionally is a vital aspect of any protective strategy. Then is how to cultivate the right mindset

Confidence and commission Cultivate tone- confidence through knowledge and training. Believe in your capability to defend yourself and maintain a positive tone- image. Projecting confidence can discourage implicit bushwhackers.

Stress operation Develop effective stress operation ways to remain calm and composed in high- pressure situations. ways similar as controlled breathing, contemplation, or visualization can help regulate feelings and promote internal clarity.

Mental Rehearsal Practice internal trial by imaging implicit hanging situations and strategizing your responses. This exercise helps to mentally prepare for colorful scripts and enhances your decision- making under stress.

Trust Your Instincts Your suspicion frequently provides precious information. Learn to trust your instincts and actaccordingly.However, take immediate action to cover yourself, If you smell peril.

Chapter 7: Goalie Training: From Novice to Netminder

Introduction:

Being a goaltender in sports like ice hockey, soccer, lacrosse, or field hockey requires a unique set of chops, dexterity, and internal fiber. The part of a goalie is vital in any platoon's success, as they're the last line of defense. Whether you are a neophyte looking to come a netminder or an aspiring goalie aiming to ameliorate your chops, this comprehensive companion will take you through the colorful aspects of goalie training. From learning the basics to advanced ways, we will explore the crucial rudiments necessary to develop into a redoubtable goalie.

learning the Basics
Before diving into advanced ways, it's essential to develop a strong foundation in the basics of goaltending. Then are some crucial aspects to concentrate on

station and Positioning launch by learning the proper station and positioning in the net. The introductory station involves having your bases shoulder- range piecemeal, knees slightly fraudulent, weight on the balls of your bases, and arms ready to reply. Positioning within the net depends on the angle of attack and the position of the elf or ball.

Hand- Eye Coordination Develop hand-eye collaboration to track the elf or ball effectively. Exercise following the line of the object with your eyes and anticipating its movement. This skill is pivotal for making timely saves and replying to shots.

response Time Quick revulsions are essential for goalies. Enhance your response time by engaging in drills that concentrate on hand and leg movement, similar as response drills with a mate or using response training tools like response balls or light boards.

Angles and Coverage Understanding angles and maximizing net content is pivotal for successful goaltending. Learn how to place yourself to cut down angles and cover as much of the net as possible. This skill minimizes the shooter's target and increases your chances of making a save.

Goaltender-Specific Chops
Being a goalie requires technical chops that differ from those of other players. Then are some crucial goaltender-specific chops to concentrate on

Glove Saves Work on your glove hand fashion to make effective saves. Exercise catching shots at different heights and pets, fastening on maintaining proper form, and snappily recovering for the coming play.

Stick Saves Master stick saves to deflect shots down from the net. Develop delicacy and control when using your stick to make saves, whether it's a poke check or a low stick save.

Butterfly fashion The butterfly fashion is a abecedarian skill for goaltenders, particularly in ice hockey. Exercise going into the butterfly position snappily and efficiently, keeping your knees together, and inclination your legs to cover the lower portion of the net.

Pad Saves and Sliding ways Work on pad saves to effectively stop shots along the ice. Exercise sliding ways, similar as the butterfly slide or the power slide, to move indirectly across the crinkle snappily.

Physical exertion
Goaltending requires physical exertion to maintain dexterity, strength, and abidance. Then are some areas to concentrate on when it comes to physical exertion

Lower Body Strength Develop lower body strength to execute explosive movements and maintain stability in the crinkle. Incorporate exercises like syllables, lunges, and plyometrics to strengthen your legs and ameliorate your power.

Core Stability A strong core is pivotal for balance and stability in thing. Include exercises like planks, Russian twists, and drug ball exercises to strengthen your core muscles.

Inflexibility Goalies need excellent inflexibility to make acrobatic saves and move fluidly in the crinkle. Regularly stretch your hips, groin, hamstrings, and shoulders to maintain and ameliorate inflexibility.

Cardiovascular Abidance Goaltenders must have sufficient cardiovascular abidance to repel the physical demands of the game. Engage in cardiovascular exercises similar as running, cycling, or interval training to ameliorate your stamina.

Mental and Psychological Preparation Goaltending requires internal fiber and cerebral medication. Then are some strategies to develop a strong mindset

Focus and attention Train your mind to stay focused throughout the game. Develop attention ways, similar as visualization or internal trial, to help you maintain focus and reply snappily to shots.

Emotional Control Goaltending can be mentally grueling , especially during high-pressure situations. Learn ways to manage stress, control feelings, and maintain countenance under pressure.

Confidence structure Confidence is crucial for a goaltender. Develop a positive tone- image by admitting your strengths and successes. Focus on perfecting your sins, but also celebrate your achievements to make confidence in your capacities.

Analytical Chops Develop the capability to dissect and learn from your performance. Review game footage, identify areas for enhancement, and set specific pretensions to enhance your chops. tone- reflection and a growth mindset are essential for nonstop development.

Practice and Game Situations
Regular practice, drills, and exposure to game situations are pivotal for goalie

development. Then are some tips to maximize your training

Drills and Repetition Engage in goaltender-specific drills that concentrate on colorful chops and scripts. Exercise shots from different angles, diversions, breakaways, and rebounds to edge your revulsions and decision- timber.

Game Simulation Emulate game situations during practice to enhance your capability to read plays and reply consequently. Work with teammates to pretend game scripts, allowing you to exercise positioning and save ways in a realistic setting.

Communication Goalies need effective communication chops to direct their teammates and coordinate protective plays. Exercise clear and terse communication with your defensemen to insure everyone is on the same runner during game situations.

Game Experience Gain as important game experience as possible. share in hassles, leagues, and events to apply your chops in real- game scripts. Game experience allows you to fine- tune your ways and acclimatize to different playing styles.

Chapter 8: Teamwork Tactics: Communication and Coordination

Introduction:

Effective Cooperation is essential for the success of any group or association. Communication and collaboration are two critical factors that contribute to the flawless functioning of a platoon. When platoon members communicate easily and coordinate their sweats efficiently, they can achieve pretensions, break problems, and negotiate tasks more effectively. In this comprehensive companion, we will explore the significance of communication and collaboration in cooperation and give practical strategies and tactics to enhance these chops.

Understanding Communication in Teamwork
Communication is the foundation of effective cooperation. It involves the exchange of information, ideas, and feedback among platoon members. Then are crucial aspects of communication that contribute to successful cooperation

Clear and Open Communication Clear and concise communication is essential to insure that dispatches are understood by all platoon members. Express ideas, opinions, and instructions in a manner that's fluently scrutable. Encourage an open terrain where platoon members feel comfortable expressing their studies and enterprises.

Active harkening Active listening is pivotal in communication. It involves giving full attention to the speaker, understanding their communication, and furnishing applicable feedback. Exercise active listening by maintaining eye contact, seesawing to indicate understanding, and rephrasing to insure appreciation.

Non-Verbal CommunicationNon-verbal cues, similar as body language, facial expressions, and tone of voice, play a significant part in communication. Pay attention tonon-verbal signals and use them effectively to convey your communication. Be apprehensive of your ownnon-verbal cues to insure thickness with your intended communication.

Feedback and Formative review Formative feedback is vital for platoon growth and enhancement. give feedback in a formative manner, fastening on specific conduct or actions rather than particular attacks. also, be open to entering feedback from platoon members and use it as an occasion to enhance your performance.

Strategies for Effective Communication To promote effective communication within a platoon, it's important to apply specific strategies and tactics. Then are some strategies to consider

Establish Clear pretensions and objects easily define platoon pretensions and objects to insure that everyone is working toward a common purpose. Communicate these pretensions to the platoon, emphasizing their significance and the anticipated issues. This clarity helps align sweats and promotes effective communication.

use Different Communication Channels Different communication channels serve different purposes. use a combination of face- to- face meetings, dispatch, phone calls, instant messaging, and collaboration tools to grease communication. Choose the applicable channel grounded on the urgency, complexity, and perceptivity of the communication.

Regular platoon Meetings record regular platoon meetings to bandy progress, address challenges, and share updates. These meetings give an occasion for platoon members to communicate their ideas, clarify prospects, and unite on problem- working. Encourage active participation and insure that all voices are heard.

Document and Share Information
Document important information, opinions, and conversations, and partake them with the platoon. This ensures that everyone is on the same runner and reduces the liability of miscommunication. Use participated platforms or design operation tools to polarize information and grease easy access for all platoon members.

Collaboration in Teamwork
Coordination involves the harmonious integration of individual sweats to achieve platoon pretensions. It ensures that platoon members are working together efficiently and effectively. Then are crucial aspects of collaboration in cooperation

Task Allocation and places easily define and allocate tasks and liabilities among platoon members grounded on their chops, moxie, and interests. Each platoon member should have a clear understanding of their part and how it contributes to the overall platoon objects. Regularly estimate and acclimate task allocation to insure an optimal distribution of workload.

Collaboration and Cooperation Foster a cooperative terrain where platoon members laboriously work together to negotiate tasks. Encourage cooperation, sharing of ideas, and using each other's strengths. Promote a sense of fellowship and foster a culture of support and respect.

Timelines and Deadlines Establish realistic timelines and deadlines for tasks and systems. easily communicate these deadlines to the platoon and insure that they're apprehensive of the precedences. Regularly cover progress and give backing when necessary to insure that tasks are completed on time.

Inflexibility and Rigidity cooperation requires inflexibility and rigidity. Encourage platoon members to be open to change, willing to acclimate their approach when demanded, and responsive to shifting precedences or unlooked-for circumstances. Effective collaboration includes the capability to acclimatize and find indispensable results when faced with challenges.

Strategies for Effective Collaboration
To enhance collaboration within a platoon, it's important to apply specific strategies and tactics. Then are some strategies to consider

Establish Clear places and liabilities easily define the places and liabilities of each platoon member. insure that everyone understands their specific benefactions and how they fit into the bigger picture. This clarity avoids confusion and streamlines collaboration.

Foster a probative terrain produce an terrain where platoon members feel comfortable seeking help and support from one another. Encourage collective backing, brainstorming, and collaboration. Foster a culture that values cooperation and emphasizes the collaborative success of the platoon.

Regular Communication and Updates Regularly communicate updates on task progress, challenges, and achievements. This ensures that platoon members are apprehensive of each other's work and can give backing when necessary. Use participated platforms or design operation tools to grease real- time updates and collaboration.

Foster Trust and Admire Trust and respect are essential for effective collaboration. Encourage open and honest communication, value different perspectives, and foster a sense of trust among platoon members. When platoon members trust and admire one another, they're more likely to unite and coordinate effectively.

prostrating Communication and Collaboration Challenges
Communication and collaboration can face challenges within a platoon. Then are strategies to overcome common obstacles

Active Problem- working Encourage the platoon to engage in active problem- working when communication or collaboration challenges arise. Encourage open dialogue, brainstorming, and collaboration to find results. Address conflicts or misconstructions instantly to help them from raising.

Clarify prospects misconstructions frequently do when prospects aren't easily communicated. Take the time to clarify prospects, both in terms of communication and collaboration. give specific guidelines, deadlines, and asked issues to insure that everyone is on the same runner.

Foster a Culture of Feedback Encourage platoon members to give feedback on communication and collaboration processes. Regularly seek input on ways to ameliorate communication and collaboration within the platoon. Be open to feedback and apply changes when necessary.

nonstop literacy and Development Encourage nonstop literacy and development in communication and collaboration chops. give openings for platoon members to attend shops, training programs, or platoon- structure exercises that concentrate on enhancing these chops.

Chapter 9: Advanced Puck Control Techniques

Introduction:

Elf control is a abecedarian skill in sports like ice hockey, field hockey, and inline hockey. It involves maintaining possession and manipulating the elf with perfection, speed, and creativity. While introductory elf control chops are essential, advanced ways take your game to the coming position. In this comprehensive companion, we will explore advanced elf control ways that can help you navigate through tight spaces, deceive opponents, and produce scoring openings. From stickhandling to fakes and dekes, we will claw into the complications of advanced elf control, furnishing practical tips and strategies to elevate your game.

Stickhandling ways
Stickhandling forms the foundation of advanced elf control. It involves manipulating the elf while maintaining control and keeping it down from opponents. Then are some advanced stickhandling ways to master

Toe Drag The toe drag is a important move that allows you to pull the elf back toward your body while maintaining control. To execute the toe drag, place the blade of your stick on top of the elf and drag it backward using the toe of the blade. This move can produce space between you and protectors, allowing for a shot or pass occasion.

Between the Legs Stickhandling the elf between your legs is a flashy move that can catch opponents off guard. To perform this fashion, position the elf slightly behind your aft bottom and use your stick to guide it through your legs to the front. learning this move adds deception and unpredictability to your elf control force.

One- Handed Stickhandling exercising one hand to control the elf demonstrates advanced stickhandling chops. By keeping one hand on the stick and using the other hand for balance and protection, you can maneuver the elf with lesser dexterity. Exercise one- handed stickhandling drills to ameliorate your control and dexterity.

Quick Hands Quick hands are essential for escaping opponents and maintaining possession. Work on developing quick and precise stickhandling movements to produce deceptive fakes and change the direction of the elf fleetly. Increase the speed and complexity of your stickhandling drills to challenge your chops and ameliorate your revulsions.

Fakes and Dekes
Fakes and dekes are advanced elf control ways used to deceive opponents and produce scoring openings. These moves involve tricking the protector by bluffing one action while executing another. Then are some effective fakes and dekes to incorporate into your elf control magazine

Shot Fakes A shot fake involves pretending to take a shot to manipulate the goaltender or defenseman. Use a quick release of the elf or a satisfying wind- up stir to make the opponent reply, creating an occasion to pass or drive to the net. learning shot fakes requires perfection and timing.

Stick Fakes Stick fakes involve moving the stick in a way that deceives the opponent. Use subtle movements to make the protector commit in one direction while you move the elf in another. This fashion can produce openings for passes or shots by dismembering the protector's positioning.

Toe Drag Deke The toe drag deke is an advanced move that combines stickhandling and deception. Perform a toe drag while groaning indirectly, pulling the elf around the protector's stick or body. This move can produce space and time for a shot or an occasion to make a pass.

Backhand Deke The cacography deke is a deceptive move that involves pulling the elf to the cacography side while groaning toward the opponent. This move can be used to shirk protectors by snappily changing the angle of attack or creating an opening for a shot on the cacography side.

guarding the Puck
Advanced elf control ways also include styles for guarding the elf from opponents' stick checks and body checks. These ways allow you to maintain possession in high- pressure situations. Then are some effective ways to cover the elf

Body Positioning Position your body between the protector and the elf to shield it from checks. Use your body to produce a hedge, keeping your bases wide for balance and stability. Keep your head up to checkup for passing options while guarding the elf.

elf Protection Moves Employ colorful moves to cover the elf, similar as the rear shoulder check, where you use your shoulder to push the protector down while maintaining control of the elf. Another effective fashion is the rear toe drag, where you pull the elf toward your cacography side while rotating your body down from the protector.

Strong Stickwork Use your stick to cover the elf by extending your reach and using it as a hedge between the elf and the protector. Keep your stick in a strong position, maintaining control while precluding opponents from dislodging the elf.

dexterity and Balance Develop dexterity and balance to cover the elf effectively. Practice quick pivots, side movements, and change of direction drills to keep protectors off balance and maintain control of the elf.

Vision and Awareness
Advanced elf control ways also bear exceptional vision and mindfulness on the ice. These chops enable you to anticipate plays, find passing lanes, and exploit scoring openings. Then is how to enhance your vision and mindfulness

Scanning the Ice Develop the habit of surveying the ice to assess the positioning of opponents, teammates, and open space. By constantly surveying the ice, you can make quick opinions and find the stylish options for passes or shots.

Peripheral Vision Train your supplemental vision to be apprehensive of players and objects in your fringe while fastening on the elf. This allows you to maintain mindfulness of the entire play, identify implicit pitfalls or openings, and make quick opinions.

Anticipating Plays Anticipating plays involves reading the movements and positioning of opponents and teammates to prognosticate their coming conduct. By studying patterns and tendencies, you can anticipate passes, block the elf, or place yourself for scoring openings.

Quick Decision- Making Advanced elf control requires quick decision- timber. Exercise making split-alternate opinions grounded on the information available to you. Develop the capability to reuse information fleetly and choose the stylish course of action.

Practice and operation
To master advanced elf control ways, harmonious practice and operation in

game situations are essential. Then are some tips for effective practice and operation

devoted Practice Sessions Set away devoted practice sessions to concentrate specifically on advanced elf control ways. Incorporate drills that replicate game situations, similar as 1- on- 1 scripts, tight space stickhandling, and small- area games.

Game Simulation Emulate game situations during practice to apply advanced elf control ways in realistic settings. Work with teammates to pretend game scripts, allowing you to exercise fakes, dekes, and guarding the elf under pressure.

videotape Analysis Review game footage or practice sessions to dissect your performance and identify areas for enhancement. Pay attention to your prosecution of advanced elf control ways and estimate their effectiveness in different situations. Use videotape analysis as a tool to upgrade your chops.

Mental Focus Advanced elf control ways bear internal focus and confidence. Develop a positive mindset, fantasize successful prosecution of ways, and approach practice and game situations with a growth mindset. Mental medication enhances your capability to apply advanced elf control ways effectively.

Chapter 10: Unleashing the Power of Power Plays

Introduction:

Power plays are a critical aspect of platoon sports similar as ice hockey, field hockey, and lacrosse. They do when one platoon has a numerical advantage due to an opponent serving a penalty. staking on power play openings can significantly cock the game in favor of the platoon with the redundant player. In this comprehensive companion, we will claw into the complications of power plays, exploring strategies, tactics, and crucial rudiments to unleash the power of power plays. From setting up the perfect conformation to executing effective plays, we will give practical tips to help you maximize your platoon's advantage and score pretensions during power plays.

Understanding the significance of Power Plays

Power plays give a unique occasion for a platoon to gain a numerical advantage over their opponents. By effectively exercising the redundant player, brigades can produce scoring openings, induce obnoxious pressure, and cock the instigation of the game. Understanding the significance of power plays is pivotal for maximizing their eventuality. Then are crucial reasons why power plays matter

Increased Scoring openings With an fresh player on the ice or field, the obnoxious platoon has further fleeting options and shooting lanes, adding the liability of scoring pretensions. Power plays allow for better elf or ball movement and further time and space to set up high- chance scoring chances.

Momentum Shift Successfully executing a power play can shift the instigation in favor of the platoon with the advantage. Scoring a thing or generating sustained obnoxious pressure can demoralize the opposing platoon and amp the platoon on the power play.

Cerebral Advantage Power plays can produce a cerebral advantage for the platoon with the redundant player. The pressure on the punished platoon increases, forcing them to defend with smaller coffers and potentially make miscalculations. The platoon on the power play can subsidize on this advantage by exploiting gaps in the defense.

Strategic Importance Power plays are critical moments in a game that can significantly impact the final outgrowth. brigades that exceed in power play situations have a advanced chance of winning games, as they can convert these openings into pretensions and gain an edge over their opponents.

Setting Up the Perfect conformation
A well- structured conformation is vital for a successful power play. It allows for effective elf movement, scoring openings, and protective content. Then are common conformations used in power plays

Marquee conformation The marquee conformation is one of the most popular power play setups. It features three players forming a high triangle in the obnoxious zone, with two players deposited near the blue line and one player posted in front of the net. This conformation allows for multiple fleeting options and shooting lanes, creating scoring openings from colorful angles.

Diamond conformation The diamond conformation involves situating one player in front of the net, two players along the half- boards, and two defensemen at the blue line. This conformation emphasizes quick elf movement, with players rotating positions to produce passing lanes and shooting openings.

Load conformation The load conformation focuses on inviting one side of the ice or field by situating multiple players in close propinquity. It aims to produce numerical superiority and exploit gaps in the defense. The players shift and rotate positions, allowing for quick passes and shots from different angles.

Box conformation The box conformation is characterized by a square- suchlike setup, with one player deposited in front of the net, two players at the sides of the net, and two defensemen at the blue line. This conformation allows for quickcross- ice passes, one- timekeepers, and defenses in front of the goaltender.

Executing Effective Power Play Plays
Effective power play plays can make the difference between a successful power play and a missed occasion. These plays involve accompanied movement, precise passes, and well- timed shots. Then are some common power play plays to consider

One- timekeeper Play The one- timekeeper play involves hot, one- touch passes to set up a player for a important shot. It requires precise timing and collaboration between the passer and the shooter. Players move the elf snappily to catch the defense and goaltender off guard, creating a high- quality scoring occasion.

Cross-Ice Pass Play Thecross-ice pass play aims to exploit the range of the ice or field. Players move the elf fleetly from one side of the conformation to the other, forcing the defense to shift and creating open end and firing lanes. This play can confuse the defense and produce scoring openings.

Net- Front Play The net- front play focuses on generating business in front of the net to produce defenses, diversions, and rebounds. Players place themselves strategically to obstruct the goaltender's view and subsidize on loose fairies in the crinkle. This play requires effective communication, timing, and quick responses to subsidize on scoring chances.

Give- and- Go Play The give- and- go play involves quick passes and player movement to produce confusion and gaps in the defense. Players change the elf fleetly, creating fleeting options and opening up shooting lanes. This play requires excellent expectation, communication, and prosecution to catch the defense off guard.

crucial rudiments for Power Play Success

To maximize the eventuality of power plays, brigades must concentrate on specific crucial rudiments. These rudiments contribute to effective power play prosecution and thing scoring. Then are essential rudiments for power play success

Puck Movement Quick and precise elf movement is pivotal in power plays. Players should move the elf efficiently, keeping the defense and goaltender guessing. This includes crisp passes, accurate firing, and maintaining possession with controlled stickhandling.

Player Movement Effective power plays involve constant player movement to produce fleeting options and openings in the defense. Players should be visionary in chancing open spaces, supporting one another, and rotating positions to confuse the defense and produce scoring openings.

Communication Clear and effective communication is vital during power plays. Players should communicate their intentions, call for passes, and give feedback to one another. This ensures that everyone is on the same runner, easing better decision- timber and prosecution.

Quick Decision- Making Power plays bear quick decision- making to subsidize on scoring openings. Players must make split-alternate judgments on whether to shoot, pass, or maintain possession. Develop the capability to read the defense, anticipate plays, and make sound opinions under pressure.

Practice and adaption
To unleash the power of power plays, brigades must devote time to exercise and acclimatize their strategies. Then are some tips for effective practice and adaption

devoted Power Play Drills Set away devoted practice time to concentrate specifically on power play scripts. Develop drills that pretend game situations, including specific power play conformations and plays. Exercise these drills regularly to upgrade timing, collaboration, and prosecution.

dissect Opponents' Penalty Payoff Strategies Study your opponents' penalty killing strategies to identify their strengths, sins, and tendencies. This analysis helps you acclimatize your power play strategies to exploit gaps in their defense and subsidize on scoring openings.

adaptations and adaption Remain adaptable during powerplays.However, be willing to make adaptations, If a particular play or conformation isn't working effectively. dissect the inflow of the game, communicate with teammates, and acclimatize your strategy consequently to maintain a competitive advantage.

videotape Analysis Review game footage of power plays to identify areas for enhancement. dissect your prosecution of conformations, plays, and decision-timber. Seek feedback from trainers and teammates to upgrade your power play strategies and enhance overall performance.

Chapter 11: Faceoffs and Forechecking: Winning Possession

Introduction:

In platoon sports similar as ice hockey, field hockey, and lacrosse, winning possession is pivotal for gaining control of the game and creating scoring openings. Two crucial rudiments that play a significant part in winning possession are faceoffs and forechecking. Faceoffs determine which platoon gains possession at the launch of play or after a cessation, while forechecking involves aggressive tactics to recapture control of the elf or ball in the obnoxious zone. In this comprehensive companion, we will claw into the complications of faceoffs and forechecking, exploring strategies, ways, and crucial rudiments to help your platoon win possession and maintain control throughout the game.

learning Faceoffs
Faceoffs are critical moments in a game, as they determine which platoon gains immediate possession of the elf or ball. Winning faceoffs requires a combination of skill, fashion, and expectation. Then are crucial aspects to concentrate on when learning faceoffs

Proper station launch by espousing a balanced and athletic station. Position your bases shoulder- range piecemeal, with one bottom slightly ahead of the other. Bend your knees, keeping your weight on the balls of your bases. This station provides stability and allows for quick movement.

Stick Positioning Position your stick on the ice in a way that provides you with maximum influence and control. trial with different hand positions on the stick to find what works best for you. Aim to have the blade of your stick flat on the ice and slightly angled toward the side you want to direct the elf or ball.

expectation Anticipating the adjudicator's movements and the opponent's tendencies is pivotal for winning faceoffs. Pay attention to the positioning and body language of your opponent to anticipate their moves. Develop the capability to reply snappily and strongly formerly the elf or ball is dropped.

fashion Variations Different sweepstakes ways can be employed depending on the situation and your strengths as a player. Some common sweepstakes ways include the forehand grip, cacography grip, and tie- up fashion. trial with these ways to find which bones
work stylish for you in different game scripts.

Communication with Teammates Communication with teammates is pivotal during faceoffs. Inform your teammates of your intended conduct and unite on strategies to support one another in winning possession. Quick and effective communication can give your platoon an advantage and produce scoring openings.

Effective Forechecking Strategies
Forechecking is the aggressive pursuit of the elf or ball in the obnoxious zone to recapture possession and produce scoring openings. It requires a combination of speed, positioning, and cooperation. Then are some effective forechecking strategies to consider

Pressure Forechecking Pressure forechecking involves putting immediate pressure on the opposing platoon's defense as soon as they gain possession of the elf or ball. The ideal is to force successions and disrupt the opponent's rout attempts. Players apply aggressive pressure in a coordinated manner, aiming to force successions and recapture control of the elf or ball.

Trap Forechecking Trap forechecking involves setting up a protective structure that forces the opposing platoon into a specific area of the ice or field. Players produce a" trap" by situating themselves strategically to limit fleeting options and force successions. This strategy requires discipline and collaboration to execute effectively.

Aggressive Pinching Aggressive pinching refers to defensemen moving up aggressively along the boards to keep the elf in the obnoxious zone. This strategy puts pressure on the opposing platoon's defense, making it delicate for them to clear the elf. Effective communication and timing between forwards and defensemen are pivotal for successful aggressive pinching.

Cycling and Support Cycling involves nonstop movement and end between forwards to maintain possession in the obnoxious zone. This strategy requires players to support one another, produce fleeting options, and maintain obnoxious pressure. By cycling the elf effectively, brigades can tire out the defense and produce scoring openings.

Reading the Play Successful forechecking requires reading the play and replying consequently. Players must anticipate the movement and decision- timber of the opponent, position themselves strategically, and apply pressure at the right time. Developing hockey sense and game mindfulness are essential for effective forechecking.

cooperation and Communication
Both faceoffs and forechecking calculate heavily on cooperation and communication. Then are some strategies to enhance cooperation and communication in winning possession

Establishing places and liabilities easily define places and liabilities for each player during faceoffs and forechecking. Assign specific tasks and positions to players grounded on their strengths and skill sets. This clarity ensures that everyone understands their part and contributes to the platoon's success in winning possession.

Quick and Effective Communication Communication is vital during faceoffs and forechecking. Players must communicate their intentions, call for the elf or ball, and give feedback to teammates. Effective communication ensures that everyone is on the same runner and can reply snappily to changing game situations.

Trust and Support Develop trust and support among teammates to encourage effective cooperation. Trust that your teammates will fulfill their places and liabilities, and support them by furnishing backing when demanded. Positive underpinning and a probative platoon culture enhance communication and cooperation.

Practice Drills and scripts Incorporate sweepstakes and forechecking drills into practice sessions to enhance cooperation and communication. Exercise colorful game scripts, including different sweepstakes situations and forechecking strategies, to make chemistry and cohesion among players.

Anticipating and Exploiting Opponents
To win possession constantly, it's important to anticipate and exploit opponents' tendencies and sins. Then are some tips to help you anticipate and exploit opponents effectively

gibing Opponents Study opponents' game footage, pay attention to their sweepstakes and rout tendencies, and dissect their forechecking strategies. Identify patterns and tendencies that can be exploited to gain an advantage.

Anticipating Breakout Plays Anticipate the opposing platoon's rout plays to position yourself effectively and disrupt their inflow. Fete passing options and routes, and apply pressure to force successions.

staking on Protective sins Identify sins in the opposing platoon's defense during forechecking. Exploit gaps, slow protectors, or inexperienced players by applying pressure in those areas. Targeting weak protective players can produce successions and scoring openings.

Adjusting and conforming Be willing to acclimate your strategies grounded on the opponent'sadjustments.However, try indispensable strategies to exploit sins or produce different pressure points, If one forechecking strategy isn't effective.

Practice and nonstop enhancement Winning possession through faceoffs and forechecking requires harmonious practice and nonstop enhancement. Then are some tips for effective practice and nonstop enhancement

devoted Faceoff Drills Set away devoted practice time for sweepstakes drills. Exercise different sweepstakes ways, anticipate opponents' movements, and pretend game scripts to enhance your sweepstakes chops.

Simulated Game Situations Emulate game situations during practice to apply sweepstakes and forechecking strategies in realistic settings. Work with teammates to pretend faceoffs and obnoxious zone play, allowing you to exercise collaboration, positioning, and decision-timber.

videotape Analysis Review game footage to dissect your performance in faceoffs and forechecking. Pay attention to your positioning, fashion, and decision- timber. Seek feedback from trainers and teammates to identify areas for enhancement and upgrade your strategies.

exertion and Speed Training Developing speed and abidance is pivotal for effective forechecking. Incorporate exertion and speed training into your exercises to ameliorate your dexterity, acceleration, and overall fitness position. Enhanced exertion allows you to sustain pressure and win further possession battles.

Chapter 12: Developing Hockey IQ: Reading the Game

Introduction:

Hockey Command, also known as hockey intelligence, refers to a player's capability to read the game, anticipate plays, make quick opinions, and execute effective strategies. It encompasses a combination of mindfulness, understanding, and suspicion that allows players to dissect the inflow of the game, exploit openings, and contribute to the platoon's success. Developing hockey Command is a nonstop process that involves observation, analysis, and practice. In this comprehensive companion, we will claw into the complications of developing hockey Command, exploring crucial rudiments, strategies, and practical tips to enhance your game reading chops and elevate your performance on the ice.

mindfulness and Observation
Developing hockey Command starts with developing a high position of mindfulness and observation chops. Being apprehensive of the game's dynamics, player positioning, and patterns of play allows you to read the game more effectively. Then are crucial aspects to concentrate on

Scanning the Ice Develop the habit of surveying the ice regularly to assess the positioning of opponents, teammates, and open space. By constantly surveying the ice, you can make quick opinions, anticipate plays, and identify implicit pitfalls or openings.

Player Positioning Pay attention to the positioning of players on the ice, both offensively and defensively. Understand the places and liabilities of each position and how they contribute to the platoon's strategy. Fete patterns and tendencies in player positioning to anticipate plays and exploit sins.

elf and Player Tracking Track the movement of the elf and players at all times. Be apprehensive of where the elf is and which players are involved in the play. This mindfulness allows you to anticipate passes, reply to changes in possession, and place yourself effectively.

Understanding Game Flow Develop an understanding of how the game flows and transitions from one phase to another. Fete shifts in instigation, changes in game tempo, and the impact of colorful game situations. This understanding enables you to acclimate your play and make opinions that contribute to the platoon's success.

assaying Game Situations
assaying game situations is a critical element of developing hockey Command. It involves assessing the environment, understanding the options available, and making informed opinions. Then are crucial rudiments to consider when assaying game situations

Offensive and Defensive Zones Understand the dynamics of the descent and protective zones. dissect the positioning of players in each zone, obnoxious strategies, protective structures, and transition plays. This analysis allows you to identify openings to support the attack, disrupt the opponent's plays, or contribute to protective content.

Power Play and Penalty Kill dissect power play and penalty kill situations to make effective opinions. Understand the strategies employed by both brigades and identify implicit sins or openings to exploit. Fete patterns in play and acclimatize your positioning and decision- making consequently.

Odd- Man Rushes Assess and reply to odd- man rushes, similar as 2- on- 1 or 3- on- 2 situations. dissect the positioning of both obnoxious and protective players, assess fleeting options, and make opinions that maximize scoring openings or protective content.

Time and Space Management Fete the significance of time and space operation in game situations. Understand when to make quick opinions, produce time and space for yourself or teammates, or apply pressure to limit the opponent's time and space. dissect the vacuity of passing options and shooting lanes, and make opinions that maximize scoring chances or protective content.

Anticipating Plays
Anticipation is a crucial element of developing hockey Command. It involves reading cues, prognosticating plays, and replying proactively. Anticipating plays allows you to be one step ahead of your opponents, produce scoring openings, and disrupt the opponent's strategies. Then are strategies to enhance expectation

Reading Body Language Pay attention to the body language of players to anticipate their coming moves. Fete cues similar as shifts in weight, stick positioning, or eye movements that indicate a player's intentions. This mindfulness allows you to reply snappily and effectively.

Predicting Passing Plays Develop the capability to prognosticate passing plays by assaying player positioning, passing lanes, and obnoxious strategies. Anticipate implicit fleeting options, cut off passing lanes, or block passes by situating yourself effectively.

Transition Play expectation Anticipate transition plays and reply consequently. Fete the inflow of play, identify implicit successions or rout openings, and acclimate your positioning to support the attack or defend against the transition.

Goalie Anticipation Develop the capability to anticipate the movements and positioning of the opposing goaltender. Read cues similar as their positioning, responses, or body language to anticipate where they might be vulnerable. This expectation allows you to exploit scoring openings by targeting specific areas of the net.

Positioning and Decision- Making
Positioning and decision- timber are critical aspects of developing hockey Command. Effective positioning allows you to be in the right place at the right time, while sound decision- making maximizes your donation to the platoon's

success. Then are strategies to enhance positioning and decision- making

Protective Positioning Understand protective positioning principles and acclimate your positioning grounded on game situations. Maintain a good gap between yourself and the opponent, angle your body to force plays to the outside, and place yourself effectively in relation to the elf and other players.

Offensive Positioning Develop an understanding of obnoxious positioning principles to produce scoring openings and support your teammates. Position yourself in areas where you can admit passes, produce fleeting options, or give defenses and diversions in front of the net.

Decision- Making Under Pressure Develop the capability to make sound opinions under pressure. Assess the available options, dissect the pitfalls and prices, and choose the option that maximizes the platoon's success. Develop countenance and confidence to make quick opinions without scrupling.

Team Systems Understanding
Understand your platoon's systems and strategies, and make opinions that align with the platoon's objects. Develop the capability to read the game within the environment of your platoon's systems, feting when to support the attack, backcheck, or apply pressure grounded on the platoon's strategies.

nonstop literacy and adaption
Developing hockey Command is an ongoing process that requires nonstop literacy and adaption. Then are strategies to grease nonstop enhancement

Game Film Analysis Review game footage to dissect your performance and decision- timber. Identify areas for enhancement, fete patterns in your play, and seek feedback from trainers and teammates. Use game film analysis as a tool for tone- reflection and refinement of your game reading chops.

Learn from Endured Players Observe and learn from educated players who demonstrate high hockey Command. Study their positioning, decision- timber, and overall game reading chops. Ask for advice and seek mentorship to accelerate your development.

Seek Feedback laboriously seek feedback from trainers and teammates regarding your game reading chops. Ask for input on areas for enhancement, strategies to enhance your decision-timber, and ways to contribute more effectively to the platoon's success.

Continual Practice Incorporate game reading exercises and drills into your practice routine. Develop small- area games or scripts that challenge your capability to read the game, anticipate plays, and make effective opinions. Regular practice allows you to upgrade your chops and develop spontaneous game reading capacities.

Chapter 13: Mental Strength and Resilience on the Ice

Introduction:

Mental strength and adaptability are essential rates for success in any sport, and ice hockey is no exception. The capability to stay focused, overcome challenges, and bounce back from lapses can make a significant difference in a player's performance on the ice. In this comprehensive companion, we will claw into the complications of developing internal strength and adaptability in ice hockey. From maintaining focus and managing feelings to embracing adversity and fostering a positive mindset, we will explore strategies and practical tips to help you make internal durability and enhance your performance on the ice.

Maintaining Focus
Maintaining focus is pivotal for peak performance in ice hockey. Distractions can hamper decision- timber, response time, and overall performance. Then are strategies to help you maintain focus

Pre-Game Routine Establish apre-game routine that helps you get into the right internal state before stepping onto the ice. This routine may include conditioning similar as visualization, harkening to music, or engaging in relaxation exercises. Stick to your routine constantly to produce a sense of familiarity and focus.

thing Setting Set specific pretensions for each game or practice session. Having clear objects helps you maintain focus and provides a sense of purpose. Break down your pretensions into manageable way and concentrate on the process rather than solely the outgrowth.

Single- Tasking Avoid multitasking on the ice. Focus on one task or play at a time, whether it's winning a sweepstakes , executing a pass, or defending against an opponent. By concentrating on the present moment, you can maximize your performance and minimize distractions.

awareness ways Exercise awareness ways to cultivate present- moment mindfulness. ways similar as deep breathing, body scanning, or fastening on a specific sensation can help anchor your attention and ameliorate attention on the ice.

Managing feelings
feelings play a significant part in ice hockey, and managing them effectively is essential for optimal performance. Then are strategies to help you manage feelings on the ice

Emotional mindfulness Develop mindfulness of your feelings and their impact on your performance. Fete how different feelings impact your decision- timber, energy position, and overall game. By understanding your emotional countries, you can more manage them.

Emotional Regulation ways Learn and practice ways to regulate your feelings.

This may involve deep breathing exercises, tone- talk, visualization, or taking a brief downtime to recapture countenance. trial with different strategies to find what works best for you.

Positive tone- Talk Use positive tone- talk to counter negative feelings and studies. Replace tone- mistrustfulness or review with declarations and encouraging statements. Remind yourself of your strengths, capabilities, and once successes to boost confidence and maintain a positive mindset.

Emotional Control in Adversity Develop the capability to maintain emotional control during grueling situations. When faced with adversity, concentrate on problem- working rather than dwelling on negative feelings. Stay collected, acclimatize to the situation, and approach challenges with a flexible mindset.

Embracing Adversity
Adversity is an ineluctable part of sports, and how you respond to it can significantly impact your performance. Embracing adversity allows you to grow, learn, and come mentally stronger. Then

are strategies to help you embrace adversity on the ice

Shift Perspective rather of viewing adversity as a negative experience, reframe it as an occasion for growth. Embrace challenges as a chance to ameliorate your chops, develop adaptability, and come a better player.

Learning Mindset Borrow a literacy mindset that focuses on gaining knowledge and experience from adversity. dissect lapses, identify areas for enhancement, and develop strategies to overcome analogous challenges in the future.

flexible Allowing Develop flexible thinking patterns that enable you to bounce back from lapses. Exercise reframing negative studies into positive or formative bones
. View failures as temporary lapses rather than endless reflections of your capacities.

Seek Support Seek support from teammates, trainers, or sports psychologists when facing adversity.

Agitating challenges and feelings with others can give precious perspectives, guidance, and stimulant.

Developing a Positive Mindset
A positive mindset is a important tool for enhancing internal strength and adaptability. It enables you to approach challenges with sanguinity and maintain provocation in the face of lapses. Then are strategies to help you develop a positive mindset on the ice

Gratitude Practice Cultivate a sense of gratefulness by fastening on the cons in your hockey trip. Regularly reflect on the aspects you appreciate, similar as probative teammates, guiding staff, or the occasion to contend. Gratitude enhances perspective and fosters a positive mindset.

Visualization use visualization ways to imagine successful plays, pretensions, or game scripts. fantasize yourself performing at your stylish and achieving your pretensions. This internal imagery reinforces positive beliefs and primes your mind for success.

Positive declarations Use positive declarations to cultivate a positive mindset. reprise empowering statements to yourself, similar as" I'm able,"" I'm flexible," or" I can overcome challenges." support positive beliefs about your capacities and eventuality.

Focus on Process Shift your focus from the outgrowth to the process. Concentrate on executing each play to the stylish of your capacities rather than solely fixating on winning or scoring. By embracing the process, you can maintain a positive mindset anyhow of the outgrowth.

Building Mental Toughness
Mental durability is the capability to remain flexible, focused, and determined in the face of adversity. Then are strategies to help you make internal durability on the ice

Grasp Challenges Seek out grueling situations and competition to make internal durability. Engage in drills or games that push you outside your comfort zone and bear internal and physical adaptability.

Practice Simulated Pressure produce practice scripts that pretend high-pressure game situations. This could involve timed drills, small- sided games, or penalty shootout simulations. By exposing yourself to simulated pressure, you can develop the internal fiber to perform under violent circumstances.

make Confidence Confidence plays a pivotal part in internal durability. Develop confidence through harmonious practice, medication, and positive tone-talk. Celebrate your achievements, both big and small, to bolster tone- belief.

Reflect and Learn After games or practices, reflect on your performance and identify areas for enhancement. Use each experience as an occasion to learn and grow. dissect your strengths and sins, and develop strategies to enhance your internal durability.

Chapter 14: Conditioning and Fitness for Pucksters

Introduction:

Ice hockey is a physically demanding sport that requires a combination of speed, dexterity, abidance, and strength. To exceed on the ice and maintain peak performance throughout the game, players need to prioritize exertion and fitness training. Proper exertion not only improves physical attributes but also enhances recovery, reduces the threat of injury, and maximizes overall game performance. In this comprehensive companion, we will claw into the complications of exertion and fitness for pucksters. From cardiovascular abidance to strength training and injury forestallment, we will explore strategies, ways, and practical tips to help you optimize your fitness position and exceed on the ice.

Cardiovascular Abidance
Cardiovascular abidance is pivotal in ice hockey as it enables players to sustain high- intensity sweats throughout the game. Then are crucial aspects to concentrate on when perfecting cardiovascular abidance

Aerobic exertion Engage in aerobic exercises similar as running, cycling, or swimming to ameliorate your cardiovascular fitness. These conditioning increase your heart rate, strengthen your heart and lungs, and enhance your capability to deliver oxygen to your muscles during violent physical exertion.

Interval Training Incorporate high- intensity interval training(HIIT) into your exercises. This involves interspersing between short bursts of maximum trouble and active recovery ages. HIIT exercises are effective in bluffing the intensity of shifts on the ice and perfecting your capability to recover snappily.

On- Ice exertion Drills Design conditioning drills that mimic game situations. Incorporate sprints, dexterity exercises, and changes of direction to replicate the demands of ice hockey. These drills will help make abidance specific to the sport and ameliorate your performance during shifts.

Cross-Training Engage incross-training conditioning that round your cardiovascular exertion. share in sports similar as soccer, basketball, or tennis that bear analogous cardiovascular demands and incorporate different movement patterns to challenge your fitness position.

Strength Training
Strength training plays a vital part in ice hockey, as it improves power, speed, and overall physical performance. Then are crucial considerations for strength training

emulsion Movements concentrate on emulsion exercises that target multiple muscle groups contemporaneously. exemplifications include syllables, deadlifts, bench presses, and pull- ups. These exercises make functional strength, ameliorate collaboration, and enhance overall power affair.

Plyometric Training Incorporate plyometric exercises into your strength training routine. Plyometrics involve explosive movements similar as jumping, bounding, and drug ball throws. These exercises ameliorate power, speed, and dexterity, which are pivotal in ice hockey.

Core Stability Strengthen your core muscles to ameliorate stability and induce power in your movements. Include exercises similar as planks, Russian twists, and drug ball rotational throws to target your core muscles effectively.

Balance and Stability Enhance your balance and stability through exercises that challenge your proprioception and collaboration. Use balance boards, stability balls, or single- leg exercises to ameliorate your on- ice stability and reduce the threat of injury.

Upper Body and Grip Strength Develop upper body and grip strength, which are essential for elf control, firing, and winning battles along the boards. Incorporate exercises similar as drive-ups, pull- ups, shoulder presses, and grip exercises like wrist ringlets and planter's walks.

Speed and dexterity
Speed and dexterity are critical in ice hockey, allowing players to outthink opponents, transition snappily, and win races for loose fairies. Then are strategies to enhance speed and dexterity

Sprint Training Include sprint training in your exertion authority to ameliorate acceleration and top speed. Perform sprints of varying distances, fastening on explosive thresholds, maintaining proper running form, and precipitously adding intensity.

Graduation Drills Incorporate graduation drills into your training to ameliorate footwork, swiftness, and dexterity. Perform exercises similar as graduation hops, side shuffles, and in- and- out drills to enhance your on- ice dexterity and change of direction capability.

Plyometric Drills Integrate plyometric exercises that emphasize explosive lower body power. Exercises like box jumps, thickset jumps, and side bounds ameliorate your capability to induce force snappily and enhance your explosive skating capability.

Change of Direction Drills Practice change of direction drills to ameliorate your capability to pivot, turn, and accelerate in different directions. Set up cones or labels and perform exercises like T- drills, figure- eight drills, and cone dexterity drills.

Reactive Training Incorporate reactive training exercises to ameliorate your capability to reply snappily to visual and audile cues. Use dexterity graduations, cones, or response balls to pretend game situations and enhance your responsiveness on the ice.

Inflexibility and Mobility
Inflexibility and mobility are essential for injury forestallment, proper movement mechanics, and range of stir

on the ice. Then are strategies to ameliorate inflexibility and mobility

Dynamic Warm-Up Prioritize a dynamic warm-up routine that includes mobility exercises and dynamic stretches. Perform exercises similar as leg swings, hipsterism circles, arm circles, and walking jabs to warm up and prepare your body for violent physical exertion.

Stretching Routine apply a regular stretching routine that focuses on major muscle groups used in ice hockey. Incorporate static stretches, fastening on areas like hips, groin, hamstrings, quadriceps, and shoulders. Hold each stretch for 15- 30 seconds and repeat multiple times.

Foam Rolling Use froth breakers or massage balls to perform tone- myofascial release ways. These ways help release muscle pressure, ameliorate blood inflow, and enhance mobility. Focus on areas like the pins, quadriceps, IT band, glutes, and upper back.

Yoga and Pilates Engage in yoga or Pilates classes to ameliorate inflexibility, balance, and core strength. These disciplines emphasize controlled movements, deep stretching, and body mindfulness, which can profit your on- ice performance and overall injury forestallment.

Recovery and Injury Prevention
Proper recovery and injury forestallment strategies are pivotal for maintaining a high position of performance and avoiding lapses. Then are strategies to prioritize recovery and injury forestallment

Rest and Sleep Allow for acceptable rest and recovery between training sessions and games. insure you get enough sleep, as it's pivotal for physical and internal recovery. Aim for 7- 9 hours of quality sleep per night.

Nutrition and Hydration Maintain a well-balanced diet that provides the necessary nutrients for optimal performance and recovery. Stay duly doused before, during, and after training sessions and games.

Active Recovery Incorporate active recovery strategies similar as light exercise, low- intensity cardio, or mobility work on rest days. This promotes blood inflow, reduces muscle soreness, and aids in the recovery process.

Injury Prevention Exercises Include injury forestallment exercises in your training routine. Focus on strengthening the muscles around your knees, hips, ankles, and shoulders to ameliorate common stability and reduce the threat of common hockey injuries.

hear to Your Body Pay attention to your body's signals and acclimate your training intensity or volumeaccordingly.However, consult with a medical professional or athletic coach to address any implicit issues, If you witness patient pain or discomfort.

Chapter 15: The Journey Continues: From Amateur to Pro

Introduction:

The transition from amateur to professional in any sport is a significant corner for athletes. It represents the capstone of times of hard work, fidelity, and perseverance. In the world of sports, particularly in hockey, the trip from amateur to professional is a rigorous and competitive process. It requires not only exceptional chops but also internal fiber, rigidity, and a grim pursuit of enhancement. In this comprehensive companion, we will claw into the complications of the trip from amateur to pro in hockey. From honing your chops and gaining exposure to making the right opinions and embracing challenges, we will explore the crucial rudiments and practical tips to navigate this transformative trip successfully.

Skill Development and Specialization
To make the transition from amateur to professional, it's essential to continuously hone your chops and specialize in specific aspects of the game. Then are crucial considerations for skill development

Identify Strengths and sins Assess your game objectively to identify your strengths and sins. Focus on enriching your strengths to an elite position while also earmarking time to perfecting areas of weakness.

Specialized Proficiency Develop specialized proficiency in abecedarian chops similar as skating, firing, passing, and elf control. Work with trainers or coaches to upgrade your fashion, insure proper mechanics, and maximize effectiveness in your movements.

Position-Specific Training If you have a preferred position, invest time in position-specific training. Develop an in-depth understanding of the conditions and nuances of your position and work on chops specific to that part.

Tactical Understanding Enhance your politic understanding of the game. Study game footage, dissect strategies and systems, and develop a keen sense of expectation and decision- timber. Understand your part within different game situations and acclimatize consequently.

Off- Ice Training Complement on- ice training with out- ice exertion and strength training. Develop a comprehensive training program that includes cardiovascular abidance, strength, power, dexterity, and inflexibility exercises to enhance your overall athleticism.

Exposure and Showcasing Your Chops
Gaining exposure and showcasing your chops are vital way in transitioning from amateur to professional. Then are strategies to increase your visibility and attract attention

share in High- Level Leagues and events Seek openings to contend in high-position leagues, events, and exhibits. Playing against strong competition increases your exposure and allows you to demonstrate your capacities against top- league opponents.

Attend Camps and Combines Attend hockey camps, combines, and showcases where scouts, agents, and platoon representatives are present. These events give openings to showcase your chops, admit feedback, and potentially get noticed by influential individualities in the hockey community.

Networking figure a network of connections within the hockey world. Attend events, join hockey associations, and engage with trainers, players, and assiduity professionals. Networking can open doors to openings, recommendations, and precious advice.

Highlight rolls and videotape Footage produce highlight rolls or collect videotape footage that showcases your chops, game highlights, and exceptional plays. Partake these rolls with scouts, agents, and brigades to demonstrate your capacities effectively.

use Social Media influence social media platforms to showcase your chops, partake your hockey trip, and connect with the hockey community. Engage with suckers, post training updates, and share game highlights to increase your visibility and attract attention.

Mental Preparedness and Rigidity
The transition from amateur to professional requires internal preparedness and rigidity. Then are strategies to develop the right mindset

Mental Resilience Cultivate internal adaptability to navigate the challenges and lapses that come with pursuing a professional career. Develop the capability to stay focused, bounce back from failures, and maintain a positive mindset.

Embrace Challenges Embrace challenges as openings for growth and enhancement. Fete that the professional position is largely competitive, and lapses are part of the trip. View challenges as learning gests and use them as provocation to push yourself further.

Mental Imagery and Visualization use internal imagery and visualization ways to prepare for the professional terrain. fantasize yourself performing at the loftiest position, handling pressure situations with countenance, and achieving success in your career.

thing Setting Set clear and attainable pretensions that align with your bournes . Break down your long- term pretensions into short- term objects and produce practicable plans to achieve them. Regularly estimate and acclimate your pretensions as you progress in your trip.

Rigidity Be adaptable and open to literacy and conforming your game. The professional position may present different systems, strategies, and styles of play. Embrace new generalities, be coachable, and acclimate your game to fit the prospects and demands of the professional terrain.

Making the Right opinions
Making the right opinions is pivotal in transitioning from amateur to

professional. Then are considerations for decision- making

Education and NCAA Assess the occasion to pursue advanced education while playing hockey. Consider the benefits of attending an NCAA program, which combines academics and calisthenics and can give a strong foundation for a professional career.

Player Agents and Representation Consider seeking representation from a estimable player agent who can guide you through the professional hockey geography. Research and elect an agent who understands your pretensions, has assiduity connections, and can negotiate contracts on your behalf.

Contract Offers and openings estimate contract offers and openings precisely. Consider factors similar as platoon character, guiding staff, playing time, position of competition, and implicit for growth. Seek advice from trusted counsels, agents, or educated players when making opinions.

Player Development Programs Assess the benefits of joining player development programs offered by professional brigades. These programs give openings to train with professionals, admit mentorship, and gain exposure to the professional terrain.

Financial Planning As you transition to the professional position, it's pivotal to develop sound fiscal planning habits. Seek guidance from fiscal counsels to manage your income, investments, and long- term fiscal security.

Professionalism and Work Ethic
Developing professionalism and a strong work heritage are essential for success at the professional position. Then are strategies to cultivate these rates

Commitment to Training devote yourself to harmonious and structured training. Develop a strong work heritage by showing up set, being immediate, and putting in the necessary trouble to ameliorate your chops and physical exertion.

Coachability and Team Player Mentality Embrace a coachable station and a platoon-first mindset. Be open to feedback, take formative review appreciatively, and demonstrate a amenability to acclimatize and learn from educated trainers and teammates.

Professional Conduct Conduct yourself professionally both on and off the ice. Show respect to trainers, teammates, opponents, officers, and suckers. Maintain a positive image and uphold high ethical norms.

Discipline and Responsibility Develop discipline and hold yourself responsible for your conduct and performance. Set high norms for yourself and strive to meet or exceed them constantly.

nonstop literacy Cultivate a mindset of nonstop literacy and enhancement. Stay informed about the rearmost developments, trends, and strategies in hockey. Seek openings to attend forums , shops, or training camps to enhance your knowledge and chops.